MW01128407

A TOLKIEN JOURNAL

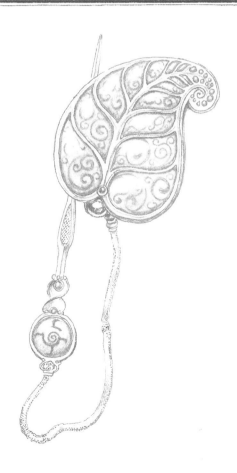

© 1978, 2002, 2012 by Running Press

Published by Running Press,
A Member of the Perseus Books Group

All rights reserved under the Pan-American
and International Copyright Conventions

Printed in the United States

*This book may not be reproduced in whole or
in part, in any form or by any means, electronic
or mechanical, including photocopying, recording,
or by any information storage and retrieval
system now known or hereafter invented,
without written permission from the publisher.*

Books published by Running Press are avail-
able at special discounts for bulk purchases
in the United States by corporations, insti-
tutions, and other organizations. For more
information, please contact the Special Mar-
kets Department at the Perseus Books Group,
2300 Chestnut Street, Suite 200, Philadelphia,
PA 19103, or call (800) 810-4145, ext. 5000,
or e-mail special.markets@perseusbooks.com.

ISBN 978-0-7624-4746-6

Library of Congress Control Number:
2012938044

9 8 7 6 5 4 3 2 1
Digit on the right indicates the number
of this printing

Cover design by Bill Jones
Edited by Geoffrey Stone
Typography: Adobe Caslon,
Penshurst, and Polyspring

Running Press Book Publishers
2300 Chestnut Street
Philadelphia, PA 19103-4371

Visit us on the web!
www.runningpress.com

A TOLKIEN JOURNAL

Being a blank book with some
curious illustrations of friends
& foes of the Nine Companions

RUNNING PRESS
PHILADELPHIA · LONDON

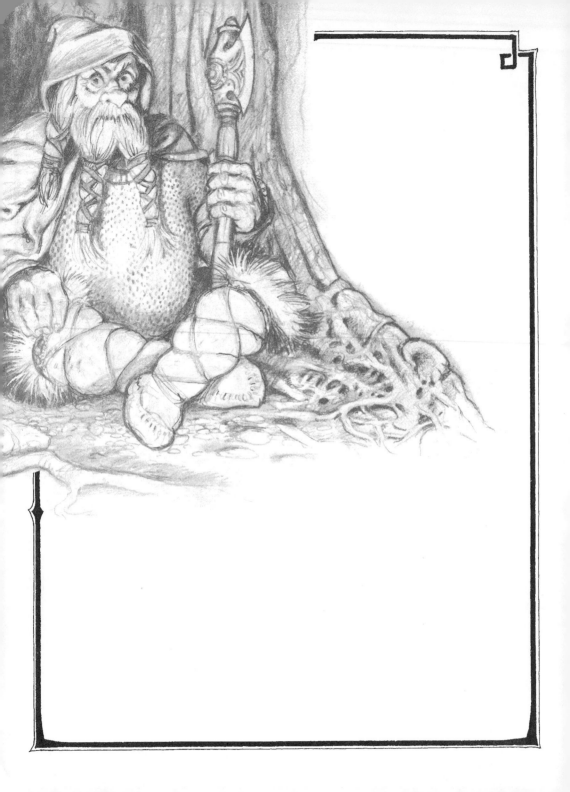

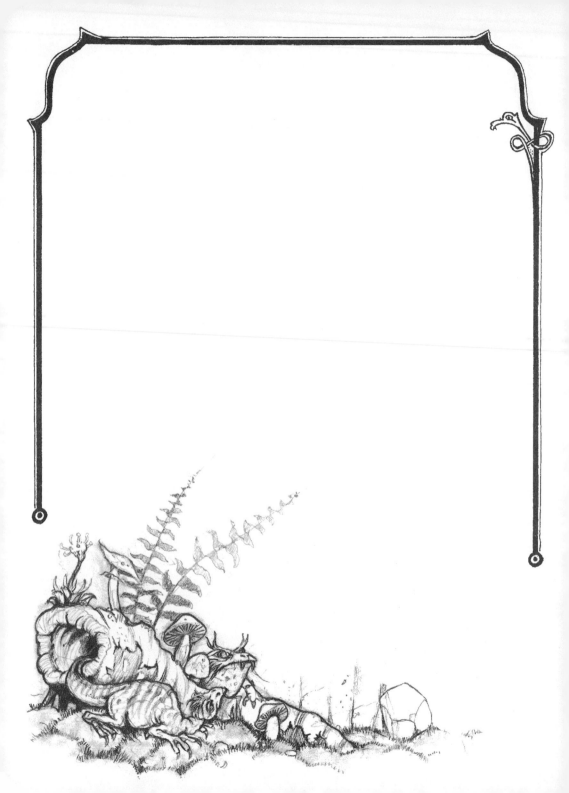

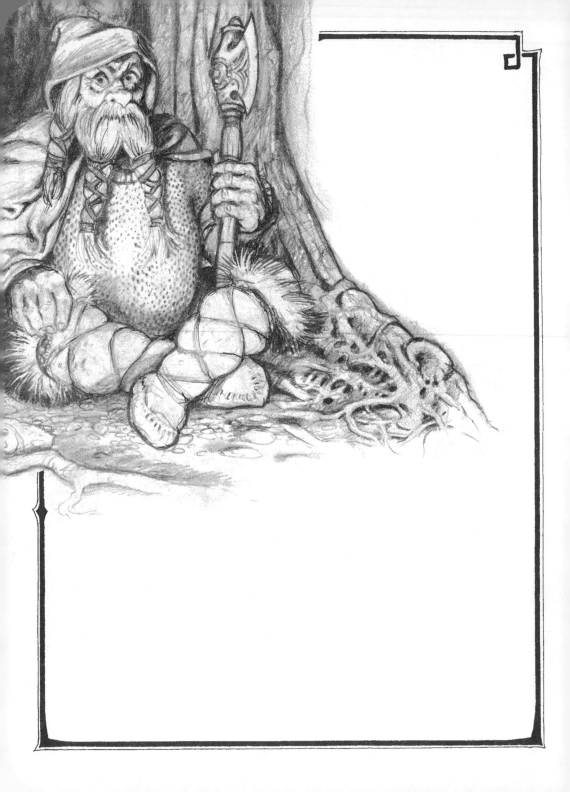